THE VILLAGE BLACKSMITH

A POEM BY HENRY WADSWORTH LONGFELLOW

To Henry

A Story of the Poem and Poet by John William Babin

John W Babin

The Village Blacksmith: A Poem by Henry Wadsworth Longfellow
Copyright © 2021 John William Babin

ISBN: 978-1-63381-253-6

Designed and produced by:
Maine Authors Publishing
12 High Street, Thomaston, Maine
www.maineauthorspublishing.com

Printed in the United States of America

SPECIAL THANKS

To Melissa Spoerl for sharing the idea with me for bringing back
The Village Blacksmith to a new generation of readers.

To Sofia Yalouris, Image Services Coordinator & Collections Technician for the Maine Historical Society for digitally remastering the original 1890 Garrett and Merrill illustrations.

To the Maine Historical Society for their support on this project.

To Lyn Smith for performing the Children's Literature Assessment.

To Rebecca Foster, who gave the manuscript the first read and edits.

To my mom, Gloria Ann Latini Babin, for reading *The Village Blacksmith* to me when I was just a child. Great memories!

ABOUT THIS BOOK

The illustrations for *The Village Blacksmith* are the original Garrett and Merrill drawings from the 1890 version of the book and were digitally enhanced. Definitions for the book come from *American Heritage Dictionary of the English Language*, fifth edition, Oxford Languages, Britannica, *Collins English Dictionary*, and Merriam-Webster. The text type for the poem *The Village Blacksmith*, The Story of the Poet text, definitions text, and the text for the poem "From My Armchair" is Minion Pro. The cover was designed by Maine Authors Publishing.

Under a spreading chestnut-tree
The village smithy stands;
The smith, a mighty man is he,
With large and **sinewy** hands;
And the muscles of his brawny arms
Are strong as iron bands.

sinewy (adj.)
1. Lean and muscular.
2. Strong and vigorous.

His hair is crisp, and black, and long,
His face is like the tan;
His **brow** is wet with honest sweat,
He earns whate'er he can,
And looks the whole world in the face,
For he owes not any man.

brow (n.)
1. The eyebrow.
2. The forehead.

Week in, week out, from morn till night,
You can hear his **bellows** blow;
You can hear him swing his heavy sledge
With measured beat and slow,
Like a **sexton** ringing the village bell,
When the evening sun is low.

bellows (n.)
1. A device with an air bag that emits a stream of air when squeezed.
2. Stoking up the fire with the bellows.

Sexton (n.)
1. a church officer or employee who takes care of the church property and performs related duties.
2. a person who takes care of a church buildings and often rings the church's bell during services.

And children coming home from school
Look in at the open door;
They love to see the flaming **forge**,
And hear the bellows roar,
And catch the burning sparks that fly
Like chaff from a threshing-floor.

forge (n.)
1. A furnace or hearth where metals are heated.
2. A workshop where pig iron is transformed into wrought iron.

He goes on Sunday to the church,
And sits among his boys;
He hears the parson pray and preach,
He hears his daughter's voice,
Singing in the village choir,
And it makes his heart **rejoice**.

rejoice (v.)
1. rejoiced, rejoicing, rejoices
(v. intr.)
2. To feel joyful; be delighted.

It sounds to him like her mother's voice,
Singing in **Paradise**!
He needs must think of her once more,
How in the grave she lies;
And with his hard, rough hand he wipes
A tear out of his eyes.

Paradise (n.)
1. A place of exceptional happiness and delight.
2. Described as a higher place, a place of contentment.

Toiling,—rejoicing,—sorrowing,
Onward through life he goes;
Each morning sees some task begin,
Each evening sees it close;
Something attempted, something done,
Has earned a night's **repose**.

repose (n.)
1. The act of resting or the state of being at rest.
2. Freedom from worry; peace of mind.
3. A state in which you are resting and feeling calm.

Thanks, thanks to thee, my worthy friend,
For the lesson thou hast taught!
Thus at the flaming forge of life
Our fortunes must be **wrought**;
Thus on its sounding anvil shaped
Each burning deed and thought.

wrought (v.)
A past tense and past participle of work.
(Adj.)
1. Shaped by hammering with a tool. Used chiefly of metals or metalwork.
2. Put together; created: a carefully wrought plan.

THE STORY OF THE POET

HENRY WADSWORTH LONGFELLOW
BY JOHN WILLIAM BABIN

Henry Wadsworth Longfellow was one of the most famous poets of the nineteenth century. He grew up in the town of Portland, Maine, with his parents, Stephen and Zilpah Longfellow, his aunt Lucia, and seven brothers and sisters. The children had a saying they would recite to tell folks their names in order of their birth: "Stephen and Henry, Elizabeth and Anne, Alex and Mary, Ellen and Sam." Henry wrote his first published poem when he was only thirteen years old. The poem was called "The Battle of Lovell's Pond," based on a story told to him by his grandfather about a 1725 battle near his home between native people and new settlers. Henry was encouraged by his parents to pursue the study of literature and was especially praised by his mother on his early works of poetry. Writing to his father about his love for poetry, Henry said, "I most eagerly aspire after future eminence in literature, my whole soul burns most ardently for it, and every thought centers in it."

As a child, Henry learned of his great-great-grandfather, who was a blacksmith in Newbury, Massachusetts. "The Village Blacksmith" was written on October 5, 1840. On October 25, 1840, Henry wrote to his father, Stephen, of the poem's future publication: "There will be a kind of ballad on a blacksmith in the next Knickerbocker, which you may consider, if you please, as a song in praise of your ancestors at Newbury." The Knickerbocker was a popular monthly magazine published in New York that featured the works of both well-known and unknown writers.

Henry was inspired by a number of blacksmith shops that he saw over the years, but especially by one that he passed daily on Brattle Street in Cambridge, Massachusetts, where he lived. The shop was owned by Dexter Pratt and sat under a beautiful chestnut tree. As the town of Cambridge, Massachusetts, grew and needed wider streets, the chestnut tree was cut down, despite the poet's protests. The children of Cambridge paid to have a chair made from the wood of the chestnut tree, and it was presented to Longfellow on his 72nd birthday with a book containing the names of each of the children. The chair is referred to as "The Children's Chair" and was designed by Longfellow's nephew, William Pitt Preble Longfellow, and built by Edgar H. Hartwell.

Longfellow was so impressed with the children's gift, he expressed his gratitude by writing the poem "From My Arm-Chair."

FROM MY ARM-CHAIR

Am I a king, that I should call my own
This splendid ebon throne?
Or by what reason, or what right divine,
Can I proclaim it mine?

Only, perhaps, by right divine of song
It may to me belong;
Only because the spreading chestnut tree
Of old was sung by me.

Well I remember it in all its prime,
When in the summer-time
The affluent foliage of its branches made
A cavern of cool shade.

There, by the blacksmith's forge, beside the street,
Its blossoms white and sweet
Enticed the bees, until it seemed alive,
And murmured like a hive.

And when the winds of autumn, with a shout,
Tossed its great arms about,
The shining chestnuts, bursting from the sheath,
Dropped to the ground beneath.

And now some fragments of its branches bare,
Shaped as a stately chair,
Have by my hearthstone found a home at last,
And whisper of the past.

The Danish king could not in all his pride
Repel the ocean tide,
But, seated in this chair, I can in rhyme
Roll back the tide of Time.

I see again, as one in vision sees,
The blossoms and the bees,
And hear the children's voices shout and call,
And the brown chestnuts fall.

I see the smithy with its fires aglow,
I hear the bellows blow,
And the shrill hammers on the anvil beat
The iron white with heat!

And thus, dear children, have ye made for me
This day a jubilee,
And to my more than three-score years and ten
Brought back my youth again.

The heart hath its own memory, like the mind,
And in it are enshrined
The precious keepsakes, into which is wrought
The giver's loving thought.

Only your love and your remembrance could
Give life to this dead wood,
And make these branches, leafless now so long,
Blossom again in song.

THE END